Unpacking
Guilt

Other books by Judith Frizlen

Words for Parents in Small Doses
Words for Teachers and Caregivers in Small Doses

Unpacking Guilt

A Mother's Journey to Freedom

by Judith Frizlen

Acknowledgements

With heartfelt thanks to my dear husband, two children,
closest friend/sister, and too many more to mention,
who have supported me in my quest to find purpose and
meaning, open-hearted living, and lots of belly laughs
so I remember not to take it all too seriously.

For practical support in turning this story into a book,
I want to thank editor Mary Oak and book designer
Chelsea Cloeter. Their skill, honesty, and enthusiasm
gave me just what I needed.

Finally, I want to acknowledge the readers of this book,
who bring my journey full circle.

CONTENTS

Prologue _____

My nest is empty, it is the first week after Easter and it's snowing. April weather does whatever it wants; winds of change blow in, lawns are sprinkled with snowdrops and colorful crocuses, and still I grab my wool socks and sweater every morning. A solo bird sings outside my window, then it's quiet again, for now.

Inside, I write, space heater warming my feet. I wear glasses to read all but the largest print, yet when I look back over my life, I see more clearly than ever before. I see beyond the inventory of gains and losses, of success and failures, to uncover the truth. It has taken years of practice to develop eyes to see what's true, to not be tricked by appearances, to get quieter, to go deeper, to let go, and to celebrate.

Today I remind myself that this is spring. Under the snow-laden ground, there is undoubtedly the activity of growth. I see the daffodils about to burst, lilies shooting up, and bulging buds on trees overhead. I sense the sap rising in them. There is more happening than can be seen with my physical eyes. There always is. I look with eyes that perceive what's true in the world outside of me, and to know the truth that lives in my soul and in my experience. In search of a way of knowing, an internal guidance and recording system, I look back to register and reconcile what life has brought me and to tell the story that gives it meaning.

The reality is that I have been lost many times, but just as many times I've been found. Getting lost in fear or despair darkens the way until inspiration allows me once again to see what is possible, to find my way, knowing I am headed where I am supposed to go. When I throw up my hands accepting that in spite of my intentions and planning I am off track, my internal guidance system kicks in or help comes along in one form or another. That's been my experience. Sometimes snow coats the early spring flowers, but they survive, the snow melts, and more flowers come. I know this to be true.

Six decades behind me, I look back with compassion. I remember as a young adult, I could see only one step ahead of me when I ventured out looking for my place in the world. My mother called me the boldest shy person she ever met, so I guess I took some risks. I struggled to find my way, looking for the life that I would recognize as my own if I could only find it or be found by it. For all the while I was looking for my life, I think my life was looking for me, too.

That sounds funny I know, but that's how I see it, and seeing it that way inspires me.

In my twenties, searching for my life's path brought me to New York City. The energy of that city matched the energy in my soul; it was an amazing laboratory for conducting experiments in living. Some experiments resulted in a picture of myself that made me (and I would venture to guess my mother) proud; others I regret because they hurt people, embarrassed me, or conflicted with prior learning about what I should do. From outward appearances, I broke the shackles of prior learning, but inwardly, the residue of guilt weighed heavily on my soul. I was not sure who I was becoming, but I was definitely not who I once was. At times, I went back home to rest and regroup. When I did, my family welcomed me, whether I was triumphant or defeated or just plain confused.

In spite of that acceptance, I carried a burden of regret about whether I was doing the right thing. It bound me to the past. When my children were young adults, I realized how stuck I was. Before I could let them go in freedom, I needed to free myself, to reconcile my past through self-forgiveness, letting go of guilt.

I remember my mother exclaiming during a chaotic moment in our family that this was not how her life was meant to be. Her life was supposed to be different. Like most things I have heard my mother say, I understand now what she was getting at. I also have renewed respect for how her generation (at least my mother and her circle) did not experience guilt or feel like bad mothers if their children made poor choices. Surely she suffered when we suffered, but she did not take on the burden of guilt. This allowed us the freedom to find our way, and we did—all eight of us. Like my mother, I have wondered how my life has gone the way it has gone. Apparently, that is something common to a midlife crisis, reconciling what did and did not happen. Today I have some understanding of that, after searching, studying, and writing. The search was guided by my questions.

If life was not how it was supposed to be, how was it supposed to be? Had someone made a big mistake or was it random and meaningless? Either picture of the world was difficult for me to swallow and not at all satisfying. I looked for a world view that would grant me courage, peace, and joy. At the very least, I needed one that would lend meaning to my life, to inspire me and make the struggles more manageable. With or without my alignment, life rolls forward with a momentum that cannot be stopped!

Regrets of the past, fears of the future, and attempts to exert control could not hold my children back when it was time to let them go. Better to grant them their freedom while staying connected like my mother did—knowing there is much they have to learn and go through on their own. I can see that now. There is no turning back to better prepare them and no forfeiting the way ahead. The only way they will be found by life is to endure getting lost, and so I must endure letting them.

My own life well lived has value. With it I demonstrate that no matter how hard, how dark, how perilous the journey is, there is always a way to move forward toward the light—to be found. There is more inside than our pasts, our mistakes, and our feelings might reveal, and hard times may be just what we need to start digging within. Compassion and self-forgiveness are key to overcoming obstacles. Inside each of us is a guide that knows the way. I've learned to know and to trust that guide and to call it karma.

Reconciling the past is part of the process of releasing it.

When I was growing up in a first-ring suburb of Buffalo in the 1960s, I had two parents, seven siblings, grandparents only blocks away, aunts, uncles, and cousins aplenty, as well as neighborhood, church, and school communities. Life flowed according to a certain rhythm or plan regardless of my likes or dislikes. Some things happened that showed me what to do; others what not to do. When I was young, it was hard to distinguish the two and I absorbed both. Later, when I found myself doing things I did not want to do, I learned to let go of what was not serving me. In the long run, I developed resilience, self-reliance, and compassion.

As a child, I thought our family was perfect, and if I look at it without judgment and consider everything as useful, we were perfect. We had even teams: four boys and four girls. Dad went to work (never missed a day in thirty years); Mom stayed home to tend the children and supported the church, school, and neighborhood at the same time. She was Catholic and lived by the strictures, not scriptures—but maybe those too in a broad sense. We were not Bible-bound in a literal way: fun was not only allowed but encouraged by my mother.

Dad's family was Presbyterian and their approach to life was simpler and quieter than the Catholic side of the family, who enjoyed fancy parties, cocktails, and poolside or beach vacations. My dad came to church with us when we were young and my mother needed help getting us dressed and packed into the station wagon, and then the church pew (up front on the left). He was handsome and stoic—the strong, silent type you saw in the movies back then. It was a façade that masked his sensitive nature; he felt things deeply and kept it in, introvert that he was. Mom was outgoing, social, and accepting.

The sun rose and set around our family unit, oversized kitchen table, plush living room carpet, and shared bedrooms and bathrooms. I can still take a lightning quick shower (though I love to languish in a hot tub). The fourth child, I was the second girl, shy and sensitive like my father but accepting like my mother. I felt things deeply and took a long time to outgrow the immature notion that the world should follow my plan, my timing, and my way. I still struggle with it at times. I'm not sure my mother knew how to deal with my introversion and propensity for exploring outside the mainstream American dream, but she let me be. She didn't reject me or even let on that she questioned the path I was on, although I am sure she did.

I was an idealist and could not understand why bad things happened, like the war and assassinations that punctuated the 60s. Since *I* knew those things were bad, why didn't the grown ups? I wondered. Why didn't they fix things? The gap between that reality and the church's, as well as pop culture's call to peace and love, was confounding to me. I felt responsible. I was unable to right these wrongs, nor, on a personal level, to avoid sexual predators or overly strict teachers, or to heal my father's soul from invisible war wounds, an unspoken but ever-present burden. All this left its mark on my developing sense of the world and myself, causing general confusion about what was what—a tangled ball of thread.

The insidious turmoil I experienced inwardly mirrored the times we were in. A sensitive soul, a seeker, my purpose became untangling the ball of confusion within. I asked deep questions and sought answers, which propelled me onto my path. Dangers associated with drinking and smoking were not public knowledge in the 1960s. Emotional boundaries were murky; there was unacknowledged, untreated alcoholism in my home and other homes in the neighborhood. It triggered shame that then inhibited emotional development, intimacy and the ability to address and solve problems. Denial dovetailed with the drinking habit and was just as pervasive, ritualistic, and compulsive. The other stuff that happened might have been dealt with if we weren't so focused on the thing or things we could not change. I adopted that same crazy-making habit: focusing on things I could not change.

My father was considered 50% disabled after World War II. Let's start there. He was overly responsible and duty-bound long before the war, but the war was definitely a tipping point for him. Imagine a sensitive, responsible young man in those conditions. He finally told us his personal war story in the later years, after watching many episodes of M*A*S*H. Before then, we knew only the story his body told. There was the scar on his chest where the bullet went in, and one on his back where half of the bullet came out. The other half of that bullet sat in his liver for the rest of his life. His fingers on one hand would not straighten again after being pelted by shrapnel; they were forever cupped, which made them good for holding change. I remember fishing a nickel from that cup to buy penny candy or a chocolate bar at the corner store.

The story he told us one evening and several times afterwards was that he and fellow soldiers were in a foxhole during a battle by the Moselle River. After deafening rounds of shelling, it was quiet. When he poked his head up to see whether they could move on, that's when he took the bullet. I've seen enough war movies and episodes of M*A*S*H to picture what happened next, beginning with triage and then transport over land and sea. A combat partner was left on the battlefield where he fell.

My father had a huge sense of regret. "That was stupid," he would say, in reference to poking his head out of the fox-hole, and he would still shake his head in disbelief fifty years later. Was that what got him drinking? He spent a year recovering in a hospital in England before sailing back home. When did the choice to have a drink become a compulsion? How else could his PTSD have been treated so he would not have been left with self-medication as the only option? Would he have lived more fully if he didn't have so much unresolved trauma?

As you can imagine, this had a big effect on my mother. She had an alcoholic father and learned about shame and denial early on. Dealing with a good man with an alcohol problem was familiar; she knew how to cope and taught us. Look good, hide what is broken, and do not ask questions that challenge the status quo. Respect external authority structures in the church, government, and society, and make sure to line up and measure up with them. Those tribal mores made for tight bonds amongst siblings, something that remains to this day. My mother's fun-loving nature made this all look workable without even giving up a good time—but I did not have her nature.

Her method did not match my inner directive or temperament. I was serious and inward, a melancholic thinker. My destiny path had to do with finding knowledge from the inside out—cultivating an inner authority, a moral compass as my guide to navigating the rushing waters of life. That shift from following a masculine authority outside myself to finding one within involved a lot of trial and error, letting go of prior learning, studying human development, and practicing a new way of being. First, I had to acknowledge what was. Easier said than done. The veils of denial, of family lore, of shame were dense and cloying—or deeply hidden, making it hard to see beyond them in order to uncover the truth.

When I was growing up in my neighborhood, children typically played for hours on end, both indoors and out. I loved to play house, especially to play the mother who got to hold the baby dolls. One of my favorites had a hard body and soft limbs; I named it after my baby brother. When it was too cold, or we had our fill of playing in the snow or exploring the neighborhood on foot or bikes, we played in the basement, which was cool year round. The doll's crib was a laundry basket and we made believe our bed was the worn leather couch in the wood-panelled recreation room with the bar and pool table.

This gave me practice in mothering and solidified my desire to become a mother one day. By the time I was old enough, I was living a bohemian artist's life—which presented challenges as far as providing a stable and healthy family home. With unresolved sexual and emotional trauma, I was disconnected from my physical body, not able to listen to its truth. My emotions were unruly and my thinking, feeling, and doing not integrated. Basically, I squandered my fertility in my 20s, although the desire to be a mother never left me.

With the birth of my daughter at the end of my third decade, I became a mother, a mother of a premature baby who was smaller than the doll I played with in childhood, breathtakingly beautiful, totally loveable, and a riddle to me at times. Her 10-week-early birth came as a surprise while we were visiting friends in the Smoky Mountains. They were also expecting and were ahead of us in alternative lifestyle planning, including homebirths, homeopathy, and organic vegetables. They had the information we were seeking.

Aside from her low weight, our daughter was perfect! With warmth and frequent feeding, she grew to full-term-baby weight in a few months. With rings of flesh, bald head, and toothless gums, she was outwardly like any other healthy baby, but the sensory environment in the hospital for 42 days had been over-stimulating and that left its mark on her nervous and digestive systems. She had cholic in the early months and persistent challenges in taking in and digesting the world, including food and other information.

When she caught up physically, I began to create the home life I had envisioned with help from our friends. We found a spacious apartment in Knoxville, Tennessee. It was a relaxed and healthy environment for her to grow in, but after a year we were missing family so we returned to our hometown of Buffalo. Under the weight of setting up life for our little family and leaving behind the artist's world of NYC, differences between my daughter's dad and I became pronounced. I was completing the course work in elementary education, creating a career choice compatible with single parenting. We separated when our daughter was two and by the time she was three, I had met my current life partner, with whom I created a secure home base for our family to grow up together and a deep well spring of love to drink from, no matter what. We live, create, struggle, and thrive together. A few years after we married, we adopted a three-year-old boy from Bogota, Colombia—another beautiful, dark-haired, green-eyed child!

When he joined our family, our son needed to learn the language, bond and attach, and assimilate into his new culture like all children—but he was already three years old. The starting place for both our children was unlike most; their first three years involved significant upheaval and setbacks, and the neural connections associated with them. I was committed to making sure their lives would work and regretted what I could not change, especially the formative first three years of life that we missed as a family.

The contrast between what was and the ideal triggered overdrive which involved too much thinking, feeling, and doing—not the model of balance I was striving for! I was stuck on the picture of the perfect birth, the perfect food, the perfect homemaker and mother archetype, the one I would and could never be. What I could do to mother my young children was to limit my work as an educator, to spend more time at home. I volunteered, taught parent-toddler programs, led seminars for teachers, and eventually became a Waldorf early childhood teacher. At that time, fortified by knowledge of best parenting practices (again the ideal), I began this general reconciliation of motherhood, of uncovering and reconciling regrets.

I discovered that regrets do not change anything, but they block acceptance—unconsciously reinforcing patterns of behavior and adding a layer of emotional chaos. Young children internalize everything in the environment; they are unable to separate themselves and understand intellectually what is happening. When adults' emotions are absorbed, they become the child's inner conflict. Later, our work is cut out for us, if we choose to do it; if we find the strength, knowledge, and space; if we stop to read the road signs along the way. Otherwise, we continue to repeat the pattern. This is the journey within, the path to freedom.

When our daughter was in her last year of high school, she got sick: ongoing stomach problems became full-blown IBS accompanied by a myriad of perplexing symptoms. Through a process of medical tests and trial and error she removed gluten and dairy from her diet, but her body experienced a healing crisis. After this setback, with both trepidation and a strong desire for independence, she ventured back into the world. She chose to take a tour of the country in a private bus driven by a family who hawked their art at music festivals. This was her own hero's journey, not mine. The illness was a setback in her independence; the trip catapulted her into the world.

When our son was in high school and got his driver's license, he explored loud music, dating, and the speed limit. I wished he would play it safer and not test the limits as I had in high school. I regretted that I had not set clear, consistent boundaries delivered with neutral affect in their early childhood years, so I could feel less compelled to do it when my children were ready to experience a wider playing field. My husband was working long hours and taking investment risks that made me nervous. I was stressed and unhappy, attached to what I wanted, regretting what I hadn't done that I now knew would have made a difference. Like a dog chasing its tail, the thought loop of regret got me nowhere but stuck.

That reminds me of the yellow, hard-plastic tape dispenser in the closet of my parents' kitchen that said, "We grow too soon old and too late smart." Perhaps I am not alone in experiencing regret about my long and arduous learning curve. How I wish I had known earlier what I now know today!

When I was approaching the end of the phase of active mothering, letting go of my children, I wanted a do-over along with a guarantee that everything would turn out okay—that my kids would be happy and healthy and that I would be regret-free, poised to enter the next phase of my life. I had some work to do, inner work. Eventually, I gave up trying to rein in my grown children (that horse left the stable already) and my husband (whose work was literally his own business). I started focusing on mastering myself—my thoughts, feelings, and actions.

I found spending time with my women friends gave me something I did not find elsewhere, beginning with acceptance. When we got together, we laughed in spite of our pain. One day, we decided to plan a trip, and the "love, light, and laughter tour" was hatched.

It was to be a tour of gardens in Scotland, and being soulful women, we knew it would be as much a tour of the external gardens as of the gardens of our hearts and souls. In search of the fountain of life that flows in a well-nourished soul, I set out to quench my parched one. I had forgotten how to laugh at life's ironies (or perhaps I never knew how) except when I was carried by my friends. I had lost the love in my own heart that flows out and boomerangs back. Being the serious, deep thinker I am, I was challenged when it comes to lightening up. I was dogged by dark thoughts, especially when I closed my eyes before falling asleep at night. Clearly, my soul was sick and needed attention. I did not know how to both allow and detach from my feelings, so they continued to show up, to get my attention as I was trying to shoo them away, all the while glaring reptilian-style at my difficulties.

Certain that there was a way to find peace, to end this inner conflict, I prepared for the journey with my friends. This journey marked the beginning of a process of finding love, light, and laughter in my soul. I took the possibility of that trip—ten glorious days with my women friends—and I used it to bookend my life. There was the time before the trip, the time after the trip, and the trip: that's the subject of this memoir. I sought a panoramic view of my past, present, and future. I turned that trip into a pilgrimage, a spiritual journey toward what I wanted in life. It wasn't that I could change my circumstances by going away, but I could retreat a little, restore a little, and initiate a practice of creating lasting change in myself while separate from the triggers that reinforced old patterns.

This wasn't the first time in my life that my desires did not match up with outcomes, but somehow at 50 years old (when I took the trip to Scotland), the barrier to accepting my mothering felt like one I couldn't get over—not without a profound change of heart. I was wracked with self-recrimination. My desire to be the perfect mother left little room for mistakes, for trusting karma, for learning as I went along. Without acceptance, I could not release the past or change the future. I longed for seeds of acceptance to grow in my soul.

A dip in the search for meaning occurs in most people around midlife; why would I be different? Raising children no longer provided meaning. The bulk of that work was done; they were now adults able to make their own decisions. I had to reconcile unexpected outcomes, make peace with myself, and choose what would provide meaning and purpose in my life going forward. That would involve not only gaining new skills, but also letting go of what was no longer working.

It's this search for meaning that brought me to deepen my spiritual studies and practices, to reawaken my spirit and understand the significance of my life's experiences. I recommitted to studying Rudolf Steiner's anthroposophy as well as the Al-Anon twelve-step program for recovering from the effects of alcoholism which impacted my childhood. In addition, I practiced yoga and meditation daily, having dabbled since I was in high school, when I began an exploration of Eastern philosophy.

Anthroposophy provides me with a compelling picture of the world and ways to enhance my humanity and experience of living. It is a conscious, scientific path of self development including practices of study and meditation. The work of Rudolf Steiner, an Austrian natural scientist, philosopher, and humanitarian, anthroposophy is both cosmic and far-reaching as well as detailed and practical. I have yet to encounter a directive in experiential learning that is as inspiring and effective. Once anthroposophy captured my imagination, I had a path to follow with as much inner work as outer work, to strive toward the potential of an incarnated human being. Awakening to this possibility heightened my awareness of shortcomings, and in that uncomfortable state I swallowed the poison of regret. Anthroposophy is a personal path toward love and freedom that encourages self examination without regret and self-recrimination—but it happens. I continue to practice.

In addition to anthroposophic study and work focused in the realm of Waldorf education, I found opportunities for social-emotional healing in Al-Anon. The twelve steps and traditions create a reliably safe place for gathering to heal from the effects of alcoholism. Serenity is the goal; learning to create an open vessel to receive it grants us something to pass forward. Like anthroposophy, it is an experiential learning process. Listening to others' stories allows me to recognize and embrace mine, standing shoulder to shoulder rather than above or below anyone. Receiving love helps me cultivate self-love. As they say in meetings, it works if you work it!

Daily practice is the key to mastery. The feminine knowledge or yin practices I have sought out emphasize connection within and learning to grow through whatever comes. Everything is useful. I did my best with the circumstances of my life and to live with the consequences of my actions. Now I know more than I did and would make different choices, but I cannot change the past. What I can do is examine it and learn from it, with the help of my friends and forces that are greater than, all around, and deep within me. Although the healing process involves focusing on ourselves, once healed, we are better able to serve others.

According to Rudolf Steiner, before I began this journey of life, I chose the experiences that would allow me to learn what I needed to learn and lead me to my purpose in life. That's how karma works; it's the only thing we take with us when we leave this world and it prepares the curriculum for our next incarnation. The people and situations that come into my life come to serve the greater good, though at times they are uncomfortable and I question whether good will prevail. This choice-making that occurs prior to our birth is quickly forgotten when we arrive amongst all the beautiful, and sometimes jarring things we encounter on Earth. We forget the spiritual contract we made to meet the people and experiences we need to meet in order to learn. To let go of the past and be ready to meet the future, it was time for me to remember that contract, to release regret, and to forgive myself.

The law of karma brings us the people and events we need, to teach us the lessons we need to learn. It is up to us to bring the will that gives us power to meet the lessons. My image of karma is that of a benevolent teacher presenting lessons that require my attention. In a world of so many distractions, getting my attention might require crisis, something that takes me away from day-to-day living. Any going forward through the muck involves yielding to the laws of karma and its cosmic record-keeping. We don't get a copy of our karmic record to consciously decide which lessons we want and in what order, but trusting its wisdom leads to knowing that things will often make sense in hindsight.

Fighting karma is an exhausting battle where nobody wins. When we resist rather than engage in the lessons that karma delivers, we are presented with the same lessons again. Ultimately, saying yes to life is easier than resisting. Saying yes does not imply liking what comes. Our opinions are beside the point when it comes to karma and if we indulge them, they can tyrannize us, slow down the process, and hide the truth. Life will always involve contrast between what is and what could be; it's an ongoing creative process.

There I was, rediscovering meaning in order to fulfill my purpose, to engage in work not yet revealed to me. I was preparing myself by cleaning up regrets, misconceptions, and self-recrimination. I would know the work was done when I gained a sense of peace, of freedom to savor life without the burden of regrets about the past or fear of the future. I sought the balance that E.B. White referred to when he wrote these words: "I get up in the morning torn between the desire to save the world or to savor it. This makes it hard to plan my day."

For all our children and mothers, we do our best with what we know and have, reflecting and re-evaluating along the way. What we learn through experience, we can learn no other way, no sooner than we learn it. When our children are grown, there is space to pause and reflect in a deeper way. Our lives are changing but they are not over. There is still mothering of adult children, of ideas, of projects, and of ourselves. In the midst of this transition, I needed to mother myself by re-creating my experience from within. To have an authentically lived life, there must be a flow of energy from the inner to the outer world.

At this point, blocked and aware, I was uncomfortable and ready for the journey. Trusting karma, I was eager to meet the people, places, and experiences that would propel me forward, if I stayed awake.

May this story remind you, dear reader, of what is important, provide a new lens for seeing the world with compassion especially toward yourself, and most of all assist you in standing in the steady and nourishing flow of the fountain of life. Our children are watching us; we are still becoming us; the world is awaiting us.

Before the Trip _____

Packing and Unpacking My Bag

How did I pack for my trip? I considered the climate and geography of our destinations in Scotland and the kinds of activities we planned to do. Rain gear. Umbrella. Warm sweater and socks. Walking shoes. Sandals. All these are required gear in Scotland in the summer. We did not plan to go out to the theater or opera or fine dining. No need for dress-up clothes.

Packing for the trip involved an inventory of my wardrobe and a shopping trip to purchase any thing that I would need. Given the trip's spiritual intention, the rest involved a soul inventory—an honest and courageous one to identify what I had and what I was looking for on the trip, what was missing. Making a list and then packing a suitcase requires objectivity; so does taking an inventory of my inner resources. What did I have that helped create freedom in my life and what did I need to acquire?

Before the quest, I recognized that I was unable to laugh, to give and receive love freely, or to simply lighten up, and knowing it in some ways made it worse. I was in a mode of self-protection, surviving by going through the motions of living, but missing what makes life worth living and craving it. As already mentioned, after much hand-wringing and frankly trying to change others, it became apparent that I could not change my circumstances without changing me. I'd reached a threshold where the fountain of life had stopped flowing; it was clogged, leaky, and sputtering and I had to do something about it, to do something about me. This moment of self-responsibility is pivotal, leading to the road less travelled, the road to freedom.

I wanted to find a way to begin anew, to wake up to the fullness of my life, circumstances being what they may. It had to be simple because I was tired. It had to work independently of what others were doing or not doing so I could be empowered. A path to the future would look different from my past. Circular thinking would be interrupted, my thoughts refreshed, leading to a new lens, a new vision, transformation.

Writing has always helped me understand life's circumstances and my inner reactions to them, especially habits or patterns. I packed a small journal and pen as well as a strong intention to write daily. By writing, I become the author of my own life, strengthening the connection to my inner authority. Traveling has also served learning in that it provides opportunities for distance, for fresh sensory impressions to trigger new thoughts and awareness. Taking my attention away from my difficulties into new terrain lets me perceive with fresh eyes and write a new story, recorded in the books of bound blank pages I fill daily.

If I can put into words whatever I am experiencing, I am able to live with it. If I cannot tell the story, I cannot assimilate what is happening and like undigested matter in my body, I react to it *allergically*, trying to reject the unwelcomed substance in any way I can find—the psychic equivalent of itching and sneezing.

The intentions of the trip, my traveling companions, and new practices gave me the hope and courage to build a new framework of thinking and feeling for a tired soul. That intention was ritualized at the Ring of Brogdar, an ancient stone site on the Island of Orkney, where I made a promise to myself. It was on that site 5,000 years ago that men and women committed to marriage for a year and a day, and if it held, they would then enter a church and commit to seven more years. Tapping into this power of commitment at that 5,000-year-old site, I promised to practice love, light, and laughter for a year and a day and to keep it alive by writing about the trip. That promise and the subsequent practices I adopted got the fountain of life flowing again and helped me realize that I had a power switch inside me all along. Sounds simple, but it is not easy. Although the journey within may be the most rewarding, it is also the longest and most arduous.

I wrote for a year and a day after the trip, and then seven years later I recommitted to writing this story, and more than a decade later I am ready to finish it. I've seen old habits die and new ones form over the years, as I have developed the strength and freedom to be of service to others. Writing this story has served me well and now it is time for it to be of service to others, but now I'm getting ahead of myself.

The trip to Scotland with three dear women friends was dubbed "the love, light, and laughter tour." Those three lovely sisters (the women and the ideals) became the corner-stone of my new practice. Being in the company of spirited women and creating a gap between day-to-day situations and my habitual reactions to them allowed me to choose all over again, to start a new practice of living.

If granted three wishes in the fairy tale of my life, I would ask for love, light, and laughter. That's what I looked for on the trip and then when I got home, sought to keep alive through writing and a process of interrupting and re-claiming my thoughts.

Whenever I got stuck—as evidenced by a loss of humor, a feeling of tightness in my heart and throat, and recurring dark thoughts—I engaged in a simple inward process. (See the appendix.) The first step is to pause, creating an opening for something new to enter. At the same time that I was looking to initiate new practices on the trip, I also had some unpacking to do, of mental and behavioral habits. In order to choose anew, a pause is necessary.

If I struggled to admit what was on the list of my self inventory, I needed only to look at my life and see myself mirrored everywhere. In my pet. In my home. In my physical body. The places in my life that triggered emotional reactions prior to the trip helped me identify and celebrate where change was happening after the trip. I knew that if I kept doing what I had always done, I would get what I had always gotten. It was only when I began to change that I was able to see better where I had been, acknowledging the contrast in circumstances before the trip with after the trip. Recognizing small changes increases the commitment to stay the course. With persistence, small changes become big changes.

In order to recognize when change occurred, I acknowledged my baseline before the trip. Objective facts keep me from falling into the victim role, taking events personally as if the world is against me. The thought that what happens is neutral and I can learn lessons from everything allows me to go forward, to grow and get unstuck. "The law of karma is neither fatalistic nor punitive; nor is man a hapless, helpless victim in its bonds" (J.P. Vaswani).

What could an oversized, unruly dog; a leak in the kitchen; and a yeast condition have to show me? A lot, it turns out. They got my attention for one. For another, they showed me my emotional reactions and stress responses. In addressing them, I could learn the things I needed to learn to enhance my humanity, to grow as a person, to do my life better. There was no separation between those outer problems and the inner state I was in. The outer problems were obvious, informative, and nearly impossible to ignore—although I tried.

Felice Means Happy

I remember the first time I saw Felice. The scene is etched in my memory. There I was, sitting quietly on the front porch reading a book. It was the last day of the teaching year and I was relishing the expansiveness of the moment, especially after being pressed by the frenzy of the end-of-school-year activities. All was right in my world—the weather, the porch, the book, and the free time I felt I had earned. I was content. Then Felice bounded out of the car and up onto the porch. I sprang up to meet her and then stood frozen while she licked my hand and my legs and wagged not only her tail but her entire torso with such exuberance that I did not know what to do. I looked up at my husband and children getting out of the car and exclaimed, "She is so big!" Big dogs are nice dogs, they told me—which had been their refrain all along, especially when I would root for a small dog. I was not at all convinced.

They picked out Felice at the S.P.C.A. after a few scouting trips. When we visited the animal shelter together, the sights and smells triggered panic about what I was getting into and subsequently hot flashes, so I told them to go without me. Although I knew they were fans of big dogs and I was less intimidated by smaller dogs that could sit on my lap or be tucked into a bag, I chose to go along for the ride and see where it would take us. I knew the mother of the house usually ends up managing the dog, but what was involved in managing a dog—in particular our dog—I did not know yet. Until then, my experience with pets involved cats only. As you may know, they require basically litter, food, water, and petting only when the cat grants you the privilege by rubbing against your leg or persistently encroaching onto your lap, no permission asked.

Fortunately, Felice was a pretty dog, a mutt with suggestions of retriever, boxer, shepherd, and Rhodesian ridgeback. A big and strong animal, she had a number tattooed inside her ear, indicating she was a rescue. She was brought to the S.P.C.A. by way of the city animal shelter. Her chest was broad and when she was excited (which was most of the time), a ridge of black hair on her back stood alert. Independent, beautiful, and stubborn—she would fit right in with our family! At the S.P.C.A., they called her Roto-rooter because of how she torqued her body like a cork screw from tail to head and back again. That vibrant motion was overpowering and nearly impossible to contain in the beginning of our relationship, starting with the first encounter on the porch. We hoped she would grow out of it or we could train it out of her and that she would not do much harm in the meantime.

That was both the outdoor and indoor behavior she expressed whenever someone approached her on the street or walked through our door. Otherwise, she would lie around sleeping and shedding, showing no particular preference for any area except perhaps the couch, the only forbidden spot. On the street, she would pull on the leash and lunge at every dog or squirrel she saw, dragging me along. She was big and powerful with a baritone bark. In spite of her happy tail-wagging, she was threatening to most people, including me, which significantly diminished my leadership skills. Given she was much stronger than me, I was utterly frustrated while walking her, powerless over her tugs, and increasingly embarrassed and perplexed.

But then, she also garnered a lot of attention on the city streets for her beauty. She had big brown eyes encircled in black. Her coloring was golden brown like a boxer and she had a little white tuft on her chest. The ridgeback line on her back highlighted the drama of her striking appearance. Some people would stop me on the street to comment on her beauty and others would cross the street before they had the chance to find out whether she was friendly or not. Her presence demanded attention. She got mine, alright; I could not ignore her and she made it impossible for me to ignore my reactions to her behavior. The more I reacted, the more confused she became and the more I reacted. There had to be a more effective dog-walking strategy than that!

My Old House

It was built in 1892 and has been a single-family home (as it is now), a rooming house for families with children in the nearby hospital, and oddly shaped apartments. It's been chopped up, the ornate dark woodwork painted over and asbestos tiles fixed to the rotting exterior wood shingles. Each owner has had ideas about how it should be and we are not the first ones who have tried to bring it back to its original grandeur. We bought it so the separate front entrance could serve as an entryway for the second floor room, which would be my husband's architectural office. The backyard was big enough to accommodate children's play and a variety of pets, gardens, and outdoor dining areas. At one point, it was home to two businesses, two adults, two children, and two cats.

When he needed more office space, and the family needed more private space, my husband found another office that was professional rather than homelike. I went back into the classroom, the cats died (we got another cat and our first dog as you now know), the children grew, and at the first writing of this memoir, one had left home. So things changed. We painted the dining room green and the front hall red. We put a computer desk and a couch in the dining room, turning it into a den and increasing the chances that we would see our son (or at least the back of his head) while the computer screen glared at him. He bopped his head to the music as he did homework or checked in with friends on social media. It was often hard to say which.

Every now and then, if I left the water running in the bathtub while I went to do something else, the back hall closet ceiling would drip. Then the kitchen ceiling started to drip, even when I hadn't been running water upstairs. We drilled a hole in the ceiling and placed a bucket under it to protect the things on the shelves from water damage.

The Christmas tree we planted up front after dragging it indoors for the first holiday in our home grew to be two stories high. We created a sports court in the backyard, replacing the children's sandbox and swing set. We built a fence in the yard to contain the dog. The ceiling in the kitchen continued to leak sporadically. Even when we had the roof repaired, the ceiling leaked; when that happened, it got my attention.

Symptoms and Severed Rings

With a leak in the kitchen ceiling and a huge, unruly dog, I felt like the little Dutch boy with his finger in the dike. It was exhausting and I did not know how to solve either problem. Overwhelmed, I shut down to conserve energy and was subsequently no longer in the flow of life. My threshold for stress was not high enough to meet the ongoing challenges in our old home and with our big, boisterous dog. My body reacted.

Like a clogged fountain, water pooled, and mold in the form of yeast overgrew in my system, expressing itself in the form of a red, prickly rash on my right hand, puffy and itchy with a white film that is yeast's trademark. I was inwardly drowning and my body started to dry out on the edges, a sort of balancing measure. The general symptoms were low energy, bloating, cloudy thinking, and that darn rash. Although these symptoms may have been underlying or chronic for some time, they were reaching an acute phase.

This might not be the most accurate medical picture of my physical health at that time, but it is a picture that engaged my imagination. I am always grateful for medical information, but to participate in my own healing process, I need to involve more than my thinking and facts about my symptoms. Otherwise, I can see the symptoms as static, whereas imaginative pictures present a storyline or script that is changing all the time. The imagination provides the possibility of what could be, whereas facts point to what is. I need both to be engaged physically, emotionally, mentally, and spiritually—involved in healing, in moving forward.

Blood work indicated that my cholesterol was high (in spite of healthy diet and exercise habits), which concerned my doctor more than it did me. I took an alternative health product to reduce it and although it is not supposed to, it affected the yeast in my system. The cholesterol stayed the same but the red rice yeast teamed up with the yeast in my body and caused it to proliferate. To make matters worse, I was consuming a lot of a fermented yeast drink to increase my energy; instead, it encouraged the yeast growth, something it was not intended to do. My body was giving me signals that something was out of balance. The rash made my fingers swell up to the point that I had to have the jeweler cut the rings off my fingers, and that definitely got my attention. I then had symptoms and severed rings.

Making a Plan

When we four women decided to travel together, we wanted to share a life's adventure, to grow experientially and to have fun. Two women were interested in taking a garden tour and the other two were celebrating fiftieth birthdays, so this was a trip born of flowers and festivity. Scotland was chosen for reasons nobody can remember but it turns out that each of us has some Scottish blood in her veins—based on family lore at least.

I collected our stories on the "love, light, and laughter

tour." Before leaving, I promised myself and my husband that I would return with my flame rekindled to get back into the flow of life, to leave behind regrets that kept me stuck in a loop in which I was not free to create or to experience anything new. Whether motivated by friendship, adventure, or healing, we were all in, each in her own way, which became more apparent as time went on.

To plan our itinerary, we came together, weaving our deeper connection. We wanted to make the trip meaningful, so we did some research to inform decisions about where we would go, how long we would stay and generally what we wanted to see. We met on Fridays for lunchtime planning sessions highlighted by a lot of laughter. Together, we named the trip, renamed ourselves for anonymity's sake, and played with ideas.

At the first luncheon, Mari served Scottish specialties including homemade shortbread. We came with our books and ideas, made a rough outline of the journey, and divided up tasks. Each of us had a city to research including the mode of traveling there by land or sea, booking accommodations, and investigating the sites we wanted to visit. We would come together on those Friday sessions as often as needed to draw up details for the trip or just to share our enthusiasm and joy in being together.

While planning, we continued discussing our work, our families, and our souls' journeys. We discovered commonalities previously unrecognized. For instance, each of us was married and had a son and a daughter, a home with a garden, and at least one animal. Ironically, our association until then involved learning about each other's inner lives more than the outer ones. We were filling in the blanks, learning about each other, ourselves, and Scotland of course.

In Love and Laughter

Findhorn was one of the places we chose to visit; it was the one that I planned. In our conversation about it, I mentioned a book written by one of the founders of the Findhorn community, and was surprised to find another woman in the group had read it as well. The book is about the marriage of spiritual and practical knowledge that blossomed into successful gardens despite the rocky, unpromising soil at Findhorn. It triggered our interest in visiting there.

Anthroposophy, the work of Rudolf Steiner, had captured my attention years earlier, and as I've mentioned already it encouraged deep investigation and study of reality. It provided the philosophical impetus for the Findhorn community. Formed in the 1960s to explore gardening, consciousness, and lifestyle alternatives, Findhorn has fabulous landscaping, year-round residents (some of whom live in trailers like the founders), ongoing workshops, several bed and breakfasts, and interesting buildings for the visitors who come from around the world to experience the community.

The bed and breakfast that stood out from the rest advertised organic food and was named after a flower, so it fit in with our gardening theme. When emailing the proprietress, we received a noteworthy reply. There were rooms available and yes, a twin room meant two beds. To sign off, the woman bestowed a blessing: in love and laughter. It struck a chord with us and the first two intentions for the trip sprung from that closing. I must add that this was before these words became a part of our popular culture, showing up on decorative items in home sections of stores, but it must have been in the air already before it got overused and lost its meaning.

Our planning meetings were both playful and productive and we tossed around Britishisms like "brilliant" and "lovely," spoken in our best version of a British accent, hoping to sound Scottish. Anyone looking for a quiet lunch in the café we met in moved to a table away from us. We laughed to reflect our practice of keeping it light, shaking our bodies to release stress and regain perspective as we faced life's challenges. Our bonds deepened and our spirits were lifted. When we we did some research, we learned that the hours of daylight are long in Scotland in the summertime. That's when we added "light" to our list of intentions for the trip. The quality of light meant more than longer days. We sought the link between inner and outer realms; we were dedicated to cultivating our inner light.

A part of the game we played was naming things. We enjoyed repeating the towns we would see, the places where we would sleep and the food we would sample. Remembering another foursome that crossed the Atlantic from Britain to America, we compared ourselves to the Beatles. We laughed about the similarities in our trip, the obvious differences, and the cultural impact of both trips. Whenever one person takes the risk to change and grow, to fulfill a purpose, it ripples out.

In this process, we held the door to recovery open for each other, and together we were a force, a whole greater than its parts. Each of us was on a quest toward wholeness, paying attention to signs along the way and offering a little help to our friends.

A Traveling Troupe

About a week before our trip, we scheduled a dinner at Audrey's. Her home is in the country where they have goats, chickens, four-wheelers, and a pond. We included our families this time, to share our intentions and plans. We wanted our loved ones to experience our enthusiasm and friendship, and then there were also some last-minute details to discuss.

Each family brought a dish. We toured the beautiful, impeccable house and farm. The children found the two

four-wheelers in short order, and although they had a few
years to go before acquiring driver's licenses, they were given
permission to take them for a ride around the loop circling
the pond. They sped over the bumps, chasing each other
until dust covered any exposed skin and all of their clothing.
Thrilled to be behind a wheel, they drove with reckless
abandon and a fearless foot on the gas pedal. With the adults
engaged in conversation, assuming someone else was paying
attention, the children egged each other on, building up
speed on the bumpy dirt path, leaving dust flying behind
them until the dinner bell rang.

The deck overlooked the pond and the setting sun.
There was a long table set up there, big enough for our four
families and the collectively prepared plates heaping with
food that we passed around. Conversations crisscrossed the
table and laughter rumbled close behind whenever humor
struck.

After dinner, the children got back on the vehicles and
the adults cleared the table, did the dishes, and continued
talking. We women discussed our itinerary, in particular the
trains we would be taking. We talked about where to buy the
rail pass, how we would pay for it, and how much currency
we would need to exchange before leaving.

We talked about the weather; we would each need an
umbrella, a rain jacket, and a warm sweater. Would it really
be that cold in Scotland in the summer? How would our

suitcases hold all of those clothes as well as the gifts we planned to purchase while there? When the topic came around to underwear and the possibility of washing them out at night if we did not want to bring enough for a fresh pair each day, one of the husbands got up, shook his head, and commented that underwear takes up so little space in a suitcase, he wondered why were we giving it any attention. He did have a point.

By the time we finished discussing underwear, we looked around the table and the men were gone. We hadn't noticed them leaving but we knew why they left. It was not only to stop the circling vehicles or watch the fish jump when they tossed food into the pond.

If you want to clear the table, talk about panties and packing, we joked. The men did not relate to our desire to communicate about anything and everything we were thinking about. It was not just about packing and panties. It was about sharing and bonding. Soon we would be spending a lot of time together. We wanted to confide in each other. We were forming a small society, a traveling troupe; we were establishing our mores. Finding the humor in things would be *de rigueur* except when tender feelings were involved and then laughter would turn to tears, another release. But that did not come up until the end of the trip when lots of used underwear and dirty laundry had accumulated in our travel bags, ready to be washed and aired out to dry.

At this time, I'll remind you of the pact I made to dedicate myself to looking for love, light, and laughter. The stories that follow are the fruits of that covenant.

The Trip

Lost and Then Found

We arrived in the Glasgow airport in the morning after an overnight flight, but our luggage did not. Delays in the airport stateside kept our flight in flux and our luggage, too. While waiting in the airport hub before the flight, we spent our time laughing, telling stories, and feeling joyous anticipation of what was to come, whatever that might be. We would accept it. Acceptance and flexibility are practices—ones that allow the letting go of plans, expectations, and desires, so we can be satisfied with what is. They are investments in a karmic account from which withdrawals can be made later. No luggage? We were up for it. The clothes on our backs, the toothbrushes (and spare panties) in our carry-on bags, and a sense of humor were all we needed.

We left our itinerary with the airline personnel and set off by train to our first destination, Fort William. The hotel was across the street from the train station so we did not get lost or drenched on that rainy evening when we alighted from the train. A shower, a warm, soft bed, and a full British breakfast made up for our lack of clean clothes. So when we went out to explore the town in the morning, we were unencumbered by luggage. The freedom of doing without was greater than the fear of losing all our best traveling clothes. Attitude is everything.

To travel to Findhorn by public transportation, after our overnight and morning adventures in Fort William, we had to switch trains in Inverness and then find a bus or a cab in Forres. While there, we were hungry; it was dinnertime and we decided to look around for a restaurant. We went down the street and found a comfortable-looking spot, much like coffee shops we are accustomed to at home with soft chairs, creative menu signage, and beautiful surroundings. But the kitchen was closed; the waitress recommended another restaurant back down the road and around the corner a ways. Off we went. When we got there, it was full, so we retraced our steps back to the first restaurant since we'd seen a sign for a restaurant near there.

After going up the road, down the road, and up the road again, we did find our restaurant. It was cozy, colorful, and entertaining—at least the chef was the latter, but that is another story. We knew we would have given up looking if we were dragging our luggage up and down the roads. Since we were unburdened by our stuff, we decided to enjoy it, to let it go. We affirmed that our luggage would find us when we needed it. In the meantime, we did not worry; we did not try to figure it out or change it.

Why let missing luggage wreck our time together or keep us from fulfilling our long-awaited plans, not only about activities but the spirit we brought to the trip, too? We had planned to eat, drink, and be merry; so we did. The quaint restaurant, the delicious food, and the colorful proprietor would have been lost if our luggage weren't. How fortunate we were to have no luggage! We surrendered to a greater plan, to a power greater than ourselves, and did what we could with the circumstances we had.

After our dinner in Forres, the waitress called a cab. After a short ride, we saw the town of Findhorn surrounding the spiritual community that drew us there. The bed and breakfast was not far from the information center where the cabdriver left us. Without luggage, door-to-door service is not necessary. We enjoyed the adventure. Although we arrived quite late, the sun had not gone down yet.

When we walked into the Sunflower Bed and Breakfast, a glance through the glass door revealed our luggage. There it was, waiting for us. Yes: it had been delivered, and there was a note on the door letting us know. That is how we were welcomed by both our new acquaintance at the bed and breakfast and our familiar things from home.

We laughed, a lighthearted gratitude bubbling up for the

joy we maintained while our luggage was gone and the joy of having our bags back. Rather than take our stuff for granted, we were happy to receive it all again. By letting go of our material gifts, we were able to receive spiritual ones and keep the material ones in perspective.

Certainly, four jet-lagged women—and this jet-lagged woman in particular—could have reacted differently in the face of losing luggage that held all the best clothes, shoes, and toiletries accumulated by middle-aged women. Instead of reacting out of fear, we responded by letting go and trusting, and that made all the difference.

Fort William could give us all it had to give. We savored the scones with clotted cream on the pedestrian way, as well as the shops and each other. It was our introduction to Scotland and we showed up for it in spite of what was missing. Besides, you can't beat the luggage delivery service!

The Psychic Chef

If you have ever been on the road and famished, you know the challenges of searching for a meal in a strange town. Hunger and fatigue have a way of intensifying emotion, making the search more difficult. Although we were hungry, fortunately we were not burdened by heavy thoughts or luggage to drag with us, so we were open to discover what lay ahead of us.

The sign over a stone arch led us into a courtyard and the small door of an Italian restaurant. There were tables outside but it was too chilly to sit there. Inside, there were about six tables, the only one free standing right in front of the waist-high door to the kitchen. The chef was there, cooking in full view of the restaurant. He greeted us warmly and we noticed his accent was not Scottish and his personality was outgoing. Given the layout, interaction was likely and we hoped for good food as well.

We ordered pasta dishes and wine, then watched our food be prepared as we shared cooking stories. When the portions of pasta arrived we knew we would not need the salad to fill us up, but we wondered aloud if they forgot it just as the waitress brought it to the table. Then we mused about whether the chef heard us or if they always served the salad after the entree.

One of the dishes was lasagna made with white beans and vegetables—delicious; I can still taste the memory of it. Warmed by the food, the wine, and the relaxing atmosphere, one of us had a hot flash—not that it took any special circumstances to induce one. She fanned her face and we laughed. Just then the chef came out of the kitchen, walked past our table on his way to the door, fanned his face and said he was having a hot flash. We blushed, laughed, and wondered how he knew.

Our conversation shifted to communication between men and women. Amongst women, we could say less and communicate more, but with men our words were often misunderstood. The chef, on the other hand, seemed to pick up on things. We fantasized about a male who would understand our feelings, our desires, and our changing needs (especially at midlife), who could cook for us as well. I smiled inwardly knowing my favorite chef and a fine meal would await me when I got home. We talked about our spouses whom we love and appreciate in spite of the struggle to communicate on occasion. Finally, we expressed gratitude for our women friends who get it, providing the balance we seek.

We asked the chef when he re-entered the restaurant if we could get a cab. "You are going to Findhorn," he stated. As we wondered again how he knew something we had not told him, he instructed the waitress to call a cab. He then told us about himself. He was from Italy and now he loves living in Scotland. His initials are JC, like another whom he compared himself to, calling himself the ugly copy. I guess he was referring to his inner self because he was not unattractive—small in stature, definitely large in spirit and presence.

Yes, we found the right restaurant, and afterwards we were sated, full of food and gratitude. The cab took us straight to Findhorn and you already know about the bed and breakfast where we arrived just before dark to find our luggage. Giddy with good fortune, we retold the tale of the psychic chef who tuned in to our table, and with each telling we laughed all over again.

No Hurry

After we discovered the bed and breakfast nestled in a circle of beautiful, uniquely designed buildings, we looked around the place. The house lay behind a trellis, a gateway that both invited guests in and defined the space as separate from the outside village. Outside the gate was the community of Findhorn with its paths for pedestrians only, except for the occasional car making a drop-off. Findhorn's spiritual community offers living and work options for residents and visitors who are seeking a life connected to the earth, the heavens, and all that lies between—a life of connection, of growth and learning.

Susan, the proprietress of the bed and breakfast, let us arrive, find our luggage and look around before she came inside to greet us after chatting with a neighbor. When she did, her presence filled the small living room and it felt familiar, like we were friends meeting again. We chatted about our travels and she told us of her journey from South America to Spain and then back home to Scotland, where she built the bed and breakfast she runs. She had a teenaged son living with her, older children who were independent, a business, artistic activity, and a connection to spirit that shone through her eyes and her warm heart.

Details about beds, bathrooms, breakfasts, and buses had to be worked out. What time would we need to have breakfast in order to catch the bus, meet the train, then get the cab that would take us to Cawdor Castle? We worked it out that we would go to the group singing and meditation before breakfast. That evening, we went for a walk around the community, unpacked, wrote in our journals, and then went to sleep. We were delighted with the origami flowers and chocolates left for us to find on our pillows at bedtime. The 5:00 AM sunrise woke us up and we were showered and ready for the early morning singing in the earth-roofed hut and then meditation down the road.

When we returned ready for breakfast, we were met by a beautifully set table both sturdy and lovely, with colorful and elegant dishware and tablecloth. Susan's paintings hung on the dining room walls. The landscapes invited our attention as much as the bowl of organic fruit on the table. The fruit was followed by porridge, served by Susan. While we ate, we rattled on about our experiences and when she finished serving us, she told us more about her life: a story lovely to listen to and not unlike ours. Each story truthfully told brings reciprocal blessings. Susan had experienced a divorce, international moves, a son's illness, and enough adversity to have an awakened consciousness and the fruits of powerful lessons.

In the course of planning the day, the next morning, and the rest of our stay one day at a time, we learned about Susan. First, we noticed her relaxed and present manner. She was either gathering up dishes or she was talking with us— not both at the same time. When she spoke, she rested her arm on a chair. The stillness of her body helped her words enter us more deeply, as they were delivered in such a focused way.

In order to serve breakfast at 7:30 AM, she got up at 5:30 AM. She mentioned why, declaring words that grabbed me, that I had not yet seriously pondered before or considered an option, although I have considered myself a fan of slow living: Susan does not rush, she said, and duly demonstrated. She gives herself plenty of time to prepare for her day, to do what she has to do so that when the time comes, she is ready to meet the day. She didn't say she was trying not to hurry, hoping to slow down, intending to give herself more space. No, she was truly living a life without rushing. Her inner tempo expressed itself as steady and strong and slow.

If a single mom running a business, creating art and a beautiful home and garden, living in a community that requires residents to park cars near the entrance and walk to their homes can live a life without hurry, there is hope. There is hope that we can meet life, be present to it and to each other, and create beauty, peace, and joy in our lives at our own pace in our own time!

To walk through life instead of running, to take time to greet neighbors, to breathe deeply, and to experience both inner and outer worlds in a connected, embodied way: that's what we were seeking. Some days we do it well; other days, not so well. We do know it as a possibility; we have experienced Susan modelling it. Susan's temperament lends itself to this pacing more naturally than others but each temperament can find balance between doing and being, focusing on goals and embracing serendipity, the pace of modern living, and our soul's pace. That is what we are going for.

Never Mind

The door opened before we reached the threshold where the innkeeper stood in worn jeans, a frilly blouse, and a fur-edged leather jacket—all of which appeared about a size too small. Her belly showed between her jeans and blouse and her curly auburn hair was untamed. Overall, she looked friendly and a bit carefree in spite of clearly being the one in charge. She opened the door, waved to the cabdriver, and checked in with a current guest who was ascending the stairs to her room. Before the guest on the stairs could respond, the innkeeper gestured for us to come in.

We stood at the bottom of the stairs while the guest explained how great the sightseeing tour of the island had been but how poor the restaurant service was. Putting an end to the matter with a sweep of her hand and the comment "never mind," the proprietress turned her attention to us, her new guests. She introduced herself, gave us the room numbers and keys, then promised to come up and see us shortly. Up the stairs we went.

We peeked in the first room. It was small and well appointed, with a bathroom next door big enough to hold a claw-foot bathtub, angled in the corner and surrounded by plenty of space. Then we went up to the third floor and checked out the larger room before deciding who would sleep where. Both rooms were crammed with furniture and collectibles, which amazingly maintained their place on the rug in spite of the slanted floors in the old building, a former mill. The small windows framed an idyllic view of the countryside with its green, rolling hills and a bubbling brook that must have provided the power for the mill when it was in operation. The place spoke of stories told and untold about Scotland and the Orkney islands, about the owner and the old mill.

On the wide window sill, there was a tray with an electric teapot and china cups. We made tea and then settled back on the beds to take in the room. The owner knocked and opened the door. She said it looked like a slumber party and then she settled herself on the edge of a chair before telling us about breakfast, telephoning, and general tourist information. Then she was off.

We were thrilled by her offer to use the phone for only 20 pence a minute since this was before internet access allowed us to connect with anyone, anywhere, anytime. Mari jumped up to make a call and nearly bumped into Frannie on her way to the door. Then she stepped aside and let Frannie go ahead, using our new motto, "never mind." Frannie called home first.

We laughed and then all practiced the expression "never mind," complete with a wave of the hand. We felt free—free to let go, free to play, free to lighten up and to laugh. From then on, whenever there was a concern about a train, finding a hotel, or any of the other possible inconveniences of traveling, we would wave a hand and say "never mind," and that would be it. We would shift our attention to something else.

Each time we spoke those two words, the flair of the bed-and-breakfast owner went along with them. She told us her story later that evening when we were exploring and found ourselves in the reading room where the wheel of the old mill stood by the stone wall. After we got comfortable, the innkeeper came in and told us that when she was a little girl, she and her grandfather would ride their horses up the road past the mill. Right above the mill was the spot where they would stop to have a little snack. Eating shortbread and sipping tea, she would look at the old mill and declare that one day she would own it.

That dream and those words became reality. After the

previous owners converted the mill into an inn, the girl who spoke her dream, now grown up, bought the business with her husband. During the day, the innkeeper continued to work at the tourist bureau, a job well matched with running an inn.

Good thing that she likes people so much, we commented. Well, yes, she agreed—except of course her ex-husband, whom she said she did not like that much. But with lightness and humor, even that subject did not bear heavily. It had the air of "never mind," since after touching on it she chose not to go any further.

Of course, we women were curious to know if she had any children. Ah yes, she said. She had had a child when she was a teenager. Told her mother he was premature—five years early, that is. But never mind, she added.

Celebrating the Light

The Orkney Islands have some of the best-preserved archeological sites in Europe; one of the islands is called the Egypt of the North. In addition to the stone circles, there are Neolithic villages and an ancient tomb, Maes Howe. From a distance, it looks like a small hill, grass-covered and curved. There is nothing else around on that barren landscape except for the visitor center; this great mound stands out against the vast expanse of sky and land. It was certainly worth waiting in line to go inside. The outer image aroused our curiosity, and in spite of what we had read, we had no prior experience to prepare us for what we would encounter in this prehistoric tomb.

Once inside, we learned that the purpose of the tomb is still unknown but what we do know is that through the opening in the entranceway, the light enters. On the winter solstice, it shines directly into the tomb, striking the back wall. What an engineering feat! How did they know how to create such a structure 5,000 years ago? These questions go unanswered but one can infer that the moment when the light begins its return was cause for celebration then as it is now. After the period of gradual descent into darkness and cold, it must have been a source of hope and joy to realize that the sun follows a pattern, and every year it will return.

Did the ancient Norsemen who populated this island until 1468 understand the significance of the winter solstice? We assume they did, since they invested so much energy in creating a site where the sun could be observed. While they were there, the Norsemen left their mark in the form of runes—like graffiti etched into the stone walls. Although much has changed since those ancient times, some things have not. The Norsemen bragged about their strength and their sexual prowess. Enough said on that topic, and no mention of names.

We are not the only ones searching for the light. Much

of human endeavor since early times has focused on finding the light we depend on for survival. For our traveling troupe, it was intentional. Being well acquainted with darkness, we searched for the light—but not the artificial kind that drives away the darkness and keeps us up at night. Darkness we've come to know plays an important role. It is in the darkness that the light that sustains us physically, emotionally, and spiritually is revealed. In this way, much like a dark womb holds the developing child, it is in darkness that we perceive the light. On the darkest day of the year the light is born anew, and in some traditions at that time we celebrate the birth of a child.

Stones and Seals

 Our tour of the Orkney Islands was great; so was our bus tour guide, Michael. We could not have traversed those distances on our own in one day. The tombs, the Stones of Stennis and the old villages spoke of history and a time before the split between spiritual and physical reality. We stood by them, touched them, and photographed them, generally experiencing the wonder of the place.

The bus ride, commentary about the sites, and the view of the countryside were enriching, but by the fifth stop, we were done and not going along with the crowd anymore. Our desire for information sated, we considered what we wanted to do next, unrestrained by the tour's agenda. We had seen and heard a lot, so when the bus brought us to another site and tourists were lining up on their way to the door, we chose to stay behind—or rather, three out of the four of us did.

Frannie forged ahead purposefully toward the door, so we called to get her attention. When our voices could not bridge the distance while we watched her stride toward the entrance, we ran closer and tried calling her again. Another tourist emerged slowly from the bus and headed toward the entrance, so we asked her to relay this message to Frannie: Meet us at the beach.

It was a stony beach, with waves crashing against the rocks. While gathering stones, we noticed sleek, black heads bobbing in the waves. We realized that we were being visited by a group of seals. Turning our gaze to the water, we watched their heads appear above the waves. First one, then another, then two more came in quite close to the shore. We stood and watched with gratitude and glee as this unexpected gift was presented.

Never having observed a seal close-up in its natural environment, I was thrilled and felt the sight completed our tour of the Orkneys. According to Scottish myths, when seals appear, they symbolize playfulness and change. The mythical selkies are both seal and human and can alternate living in or out of the water depending on which form they take. I thought about the qualities of seals, how the water beads on their skin and flows off their backs. Their movements are fluid as they move in and around the rocks.

We were charmed by them; they inspired our imaginations. I pictured a coat of protection on my skin, the grace to move in a way that is playful and fluid, and the ability to provide delight just by showing up. The spirit of the Orkneys had worked on us; we allowed for spontaneity, nature, and imagination. We brought stones back to the inn, where each of us fashioned her own Standing Stones of Stennis. Recreating a moment, we connected to our prehistoric brethren and our awakened spirits. What if we had gone inside with the tour? I suppose the stones and seals would not have been missed, but that niggling feeling that there is more available when we listen to our inner guide, that an opportunity came and went, may have dampened our sense of freedom, of joy, of peace—or maybe we would simply have missed the fun of seeing seals at the shore and an opportunity to write our own story.

Today—as opposed to 2,500 BC, when the Standing Stones of Stennis were erected—the physical and spiritual worlds are not melded in a way that we experience them collectively and unconsciously. No, in this era, our individual spirits harken to us so we can find the way to reunite the physical and spiritual worlds, if we have the will to hear the call.

The outcome of our choice to visit the beach was an awakening of wonder, allowing space for playfulness and integration of the sites we had seen. We never regretted what we missed, nor can I remember the name of the site. Instead, we each had twelve stones and photographs of four seals. It was a moment of choice, where by chance—or, I prefer to think, by conscious cooperation with forces of nature—we were provided with a lasting memory.

The Middle of the Boat

The Orkney Islands can be reached only by boat or plane. We took the ferry and sat on the top floor for the ninety-minute ride to the island. From there we could easily access the deck for taking in the impressive cliffs, sea birds, sky, and waves. There were many vacationing Scots on the boat; we chatted with a few, took pictures, and got a bit seasick.

It helped to go outside; perhaps the wind and the sights were a distraction from the queasiness in our stomachs. Surely it beat sitting inside and wondering if we would get sick. When we arrived on the island, we joyfully stood on solid ground and then travelled by cab to the bed and breakfast, viewing the water from the land.

When we spoke to people we met on the island, they wished us well in our sightseeing and a smooth crossing on our way back to the mainland. The weather was mild on our way over, but in spite of the clear skies overhead, the sea was rough. We started watching the weather for the return trip. For sightseeing, it was ideal—cool with clear skies. The forecast for the day we were crossing again, though, was rain. We assumed that rain implied rough waters, a rocky ride, and more seasickness.

Yes: the forecast was right, and the morning of our departure it was pouring rain when we boarded the boat. It was our first rainy day since we arrived in Scotland, even though rainy summer days are typical there. We claimed that we brought the sunshine with us, so we were surprised (as if we believed our fantasy). How could it rain now?

Our itinerary that day was tight, leaving little time in the morning to travel from the bed and breakfast to the ferry to the mainland, and from there to the train station. We relied on the cab drivers, who promised to get us there on time. While waiting for one, we ate a light breakfast, so as to have little to lose if we got sick on the boat. The cab driver arrived while we were at the breakfast table. Never mind, we were ready to go.

We loaded our bags and shook off the raindrops before getting in the cab. We asked the cab driver about crossing to the mainland and he said he had done it a few times, although he preferred to stay on the island. The island culture is a celebration of nature, and its ruggedness contrasted with our concept of modern living. He had a commonsensical suggestion for us: Go downstairs and sit in the middle. There we would be protected from the rocking of the boat. It sounded like good general advice: Stay centered while crossing stormy seas. A sign in one of the shops on shore reads: "Rough seas are what a skilled sailor makes." It was true for life's journey as well; we chose to stay in the center and were prepared for the worst.

We found a table, got a cup of coffee, and then relaxed all the way to the other side. This rainy crossing was calmer, not as windy as the first crossing when the sky was clear. The weather did not matter, though, because now we knew the secret.

The time passed quickly, and when we arrived on the other side the next cab driver was waiting to take us to the train station in Forres. We waited on the platform briefly for the train to Inverness, and on that ride we enjoyed the fine lunch that we purchased at the port, including the best chocolate-covered ginger biscuits I have ever eaten. I have been on the search for them ever since.

Mind the Gap

To the tip of mainland Scotland and back down again, we rode the train. Before the train came to a stop in a station, they would announce this warning: "Mind the gap when alighting from the train." The expression amused us, being accustomed to the cautionary phrase "watch your step."

"Mind the gap" was new to us. It was not about action, but about awareness. It was not about the positive space, but the negative—the gap, or the place in between two spaces. That's where we were hovering while on vacation, in the period of time between life before our journey and life after—a place where awareness was heightened due to the newness of our experiences. In that place of pause, perceptions come in a fresh way, illuminating our thoughts.

To mind the gap is to take note of where we are and where we are going. How many accidents could I have avoided if I remembered to mind the gap before taking a step? This awareness is about being present—present to our bodies in space. From that awareness comes the knowledge of the next right thing to do. It's the space where we create and recreate what is. It's a practice; the more we do it, the more we remember to do it.

Awareness is about more than being open to stimulus; it's about filtering the stimulus. At any given time, there is much more sensory information than we can take in and process. Our focus or purpose increases the ability to filter out the information we do not need, that is not in alignment with our intentions. A generally useful purpose is to at least do no harm. For example, to step safely onto the platform when getting off the train, to speak only kind and helpful words, to care for ourselves, are purposes in alignment with doing no harm. When we focus on our purpose, instead of an overload of sensory information and thoughts, we take in what is useful and filter out the rest.

We women had experience in refining or redefining our awareness. Each of us was once absorbed in codependent behaviors that led to overwhelm. When we focused on what others were doing—something we could not change—we took in information that we could not use, and often forgot to pay attention to what was useful, what was ours to do. This kind of awareness did not bring us closer to the goal of creating peace and joy in our lives. When we came together, we were ready to take responsibility for our actions, our feelings, and our thoughts, and to know how they were impacting our lives. We listened to others' stories and examined our lives to become aware of the presence of a higher power that we could trust enough to let go.

Physicists tell us that our bodies—in fact, the universe—is made up of a lot of space, of air, of nothingness. This picture of a power that is unlimited, clearly greater than me, is one I can embrace. It is one that is vast, full of creative potential and space for a future that does not look like the past. I trust there is an opening for change when I stop, create a gap, and make room for something greater than me. In order to stop filling the space with habitual thoughts, feelings, and actions, I need to become aware of them first.

Mind the gap, the conductor said before the doors

opened. Stop. Think. Choose. Take one step at a time. These are slogans for the Al-Anon recovery program. They slow us down so we can avoid the habit of reacting and living unconsciously. Before we brought ourselves to the tables of recovery, we forged ahead no matter what until we were too tired and could not do it anymore. Now we know we have choices. What a relief from the exhaustion of resisting and reacting!

Awareness that the old way of operating is not working is called hitting bottom. It provides the pause, the gap, an opportunity to put an end to the old and make room for the new. Without a gap, there is no opening that makes room for choice and opportunity for change.

Mind the gap, so you land safely on the platform when you step off the train. Mindfulness of the space within and around you keeps you informed and aware of an expansiveness of space. Focusing on your goal makes it more likely that you will achieve it. In that space of awareness and focus, transformation may occur, moments of freedom are possible. Mind the gap when journeying through life.

Look Right

In the British Isles, as you may already know, cars drive on the left side of the road; so when you cross the street on foot, you need to look to the right first, or a car might surprise you. Since most pedestrians visiting Britain are trained to look left first when crossing the road, there is a sign with big block letters on the road that says, "Look right." Like "Mind the gap," this direction wakes us up, when we might have been asleep before.

That bold reminder assumes the common practice of stopping at the curb before stepping off onto the street. We stop to read the signs, remember the traffic rules, look for cars, and act accordingly. Habits are not easy to break; they are behaviors that have been practiced enough to be automatic, so they are no longer conscious. What happens when we need to replace a habit with conscious action? That involves being a beginner, stopping and thinking before acting; it involves waking up.

How often are we functioning on automatic pilot as far as our lives go? Like zombies, we can carry on in a way that obscures options and veils awareness. Crossing the street in Scotland gave us a wake-up call. Ding, ding, ding, a trolley bell let us know when we stepped off the curb without thinking. Come to think of it, the vacation in general was an exercise in mindfulness, an opportunity to wake up to habitual behaviors, feelings, and thoughts, an adventure outside our daily routines.

The experience of being in the company of women who cared for themselves and each other, being away from spouses and children, work and routines, gave room for pause. In that pause, we could arrest habits and look right. If these habits are not working, what would make my life and my relationships work right?

Each of us was grieving the loss of a dream—the loss of many dreams, for life does not adapt itself to our desires if we are not satisfied. It presents itself on its own terms, in keeping with karma. Thoughts and feelings of dissatisfaction affect our physical, emotional, and spiritual well-being, our relationships and our peace of mind. Grieving is essential; it is a part of life. But either extreme—dramatizing or repressing emotion—can be a habit. Emotional imbalance or bouncing between extremes is a pattern that aligns with codependence. We women became aware of our emotional patterns and came together to break them, pulling each other up as we went along.

The tricky thing about habits is that in order for them to become visible, one must acknowledge them objectively without attachment or judgment. Then they can be unlearned and replaced by new habits. On a chilly, drizzling morning in Glasgow near the end of the trip, surrounded by supportive women and flowers, I woke up. It was in the botanical gardens across the street from our hotel. What I saw amongst the flowers was that I was choosing to shut down in my grief, that I was not sharing myself or showing up for my life much of the time. I was exaggerating difficulties, taking on others' problems, and indulging in self-pity rather than sitting with the feelings and letting them pass through me.

My head was in turmoil; there was conflict in the group, and so I sat on a bench and penned a poem on paper torn from a travel brochure. I wanted to connect to my heart and to look right toward the light before going on with the day. There was a woman dressed in black, walking with her head down and her hands in her pockets. She mirrored what I was feeling.

Grief in the Glasgow Gardens

I saw you walking in the gardens, rain hat pulled low, hands deep in black pockets.

I wondered if you too carry sorrow deep in your bones.

If you seed it with each thought layered on top of the garden's glory.

Or do you walk in freedom, choosing your path and thoughts?

Each step an issue for the dream you grieve to gracefully whither

And for new dreams to grow and blossom in your garden bed?

Have you made up your mind, dear woman?

On this gray Glasgow morning, I know I have made up mine.

Bird Call

While we explored Scottish towns together, we heard many stories. Frannie told one about another trip to Scotland. Many years earlier, she and her brother had travelled to the British Isles, where the sound of seagulls caught their attention right away. Wherever they went on the islands, there were seagulls. Being young and carefree, they imitated the seagulls' cry. "Caw, caw, caw," they would call out, blending in with the birds.

Hearing the story, we laughed and uttered a few gull cries of our own, but the purpose of the story did not reveal itself until later. When the need arose, we harkened the travelers' tenet to stick together like, well, birds of a feather. If the group splits up accidentally when one of us wanders off, then there must be a plan for finding each other—possibly a designated meeting place. Even if we lose sight of each other, we need a way to call each other back, to gather the group.

On our first day in Scotland, we roamed the pedestrian way in Fort William. It took us past shops and cafes, awakening our senses to the land. We sampled scones with clotted cream and shopped for sturdy walking shoes. We were never far from the water. Yes, everywhere we went, the sound of gulls reminded us of their presence and the story Frannie told. Surely, we wanted to join the gulls in their cry.

"Caw, caw, caw," we called out with glee. We were going to be together in Scotland for ten days and we were not going to hold back. We knew no one but each other. We would revel in the sensory experience, our spiritual connection, and everything that would come our way. When one ventured away from the group, we "cawed" for her to come back. The cry would rise above the din of the crowds, higher in pitch and volume, catching the attention of the one who wandered out of sight but within hearing distance of the group.

Wherever we were, even in Edinburgh during the packed Fringe Festival, we were reunited by a seagull cry, smiling lips, and laughing eyes. We were free to wander off knowing that there was a sound that would call us back. Scottish ambience, the preponderance of gulls, and our anonymity gave us the freedom to caw like a bird.

We discovered our group identity and also our differences on the trip. Although we had so much in common, our differences in temperament were made clear, shown by our approaches to life and ways of pursuing a goal. There was something whole and complete when we worked together. Like the four elements of the earth, we balanced each other.

Humans carry predominantly one of the four elements within us. There is a water element in Audrey; she goes with the flow, enjoying sensory experiences and forming herself to any situation like a creek rushing over and around rocks. She helped the group to let go and accept whatever came. A fire burns in Mari and she was determined to keep the group on time for the trains. When we needed a scout to go ahead and find a hotel, she was ready and willing. She kept the group on track. Frannie is airy, so she enlivened the train rides with jokes and would engage in conversations with people we met. She brought levity. There I was, negotiating a rough patch; I balanced the lightness with gravity. I would slow us down to take in less, to acknowledge what was happening, and to write about our experiences so we would remember them later. With the weight of the promise to rekindle my inner light, I needed to pay attention to what we saw and experienced as well as the more esoteric aspects of the trip.

We were each in our own way seeking the fountain of love, light, and laughter, approaching it according to our temperaments and life's circumstances at the time. Audrey was walking with a steady step, Mari was running, Frannie was skipping along, and I was crawling to the fountain. That's how it was, and in that way we did not trip over each other. We led with our individual strengths.

When we returned to the U.S., our community disbanded and our group mores with it. One of us cawed in the Philadelphia airport and the rest pretended not to hear or shot a look of embarrassment. The Scottish charm had been broken; our time together was up.

After the trip we were going to go our separate ways and return to the world of phones, lunch meetings, and occasional gatherings. When we were back in a place where we knew our way around, we were less dependent on each other. But we know that if we enter terrain that is new, challenging or in any way difficult to negotiate alone, we can call out to each other for support. Maybe that is why the gulls caw; they rely on each other, too.

After the Trip _____

When the trip was over, it was time to bring the joy and wisdom found on the journey, to integrate it into my daily life. A candle was lit and I wanted to keep it burning in my soul. I found that I could grieve and let go of regret, forgive myself, and live more fully one moment at a time. When I got off track I could return to the practice.

That is what I have found in the love, light, and laughter tour and that is the story I have to tell. In sharing it, I place my flag on top of a mountain that was challenging to climb. I get to keep what I found on the way by showing others what is possible. Suffering is what led to the search and meaning is what defined the path. When I can put into words whatever I am experiencing, I am able to live with it.

Do I wish that I had learned lessons earlier? I often do, much like I wish the sun would shine when it is cloudy, but I cannot change the weather and I cannot change my past. What I can do is change how I think about it. I can let go of the habit of trying to change the things I cannot change. My disappointment about unfulfilled wishes and my self-deprecating judgments do not rise from my higher self. They need to be acknowledged, but not given authority to determine my thoughts, feelings, and actions.

Like passing clouds, they appear and disappear. I can observe them without attaching to them. Instead, I engage in practices to strengthen my higher self, like meditation, yoga, and the love, light, and laughter exercise. They are a part of my daily life and allow me to see life from above the clouds when necessary.

I am still challenged; there are still lessons to learn. Yet I am able to detach, feel gratitude, and learn most of the time. What has happened with my pet, my health, and my home has been acknowledged, and new goals and challenges have presented themselves.

This is the end of the story of striving to digest difficult matter as far as my regrets as a mother, and to be satisfied with who I am, what I have done, and what I have. I became aware of how much I needed to do this before the trip to Scotland. When I returned, I observed my struggle to re-enter my life, my lack of acceptance of it. Since I could not get a whole new life, I needed a new perception of the one I had. In spite of troubling circumstances, it was time for more love, light, and laughter. In loving, I could open my heart to receiving love and experience the beauty of life. In the light, I could grow in my understanding of truth. By laughing, I could let go of the pain, making room to find goodness.

In order to improve my relationship to my dog, my house, and my body, I engaged in exercises to increase my inner authority and thus my effectiveness in the outer world. Accepting responsibility for whatever was in my life, I trusted that it was there for a reason and I set to work re-training my thoughts.

I remembered a verse by Rudolf Steiner, the founder of anthroposophy, and recited it regularly. By saying this verse, I focused on ideals that improve my life and allow me to have meaningful purpose, connecting with forces beyond the personal, beyond the material.

> *Let wisdom shine through me.*
> *Love glow in me.*
> *Strength uplift me.*
> *That in me may arise*
> *A helper of humanity.*
> *A servant, selfless and true.*

I found wisdom in my ever renewable, light-seeking thoughts. Love grew in my heart until it was full, and strength came from cultivating humor. With practice, I was able to laugh, especially at myself. Believe me, I am guaranteed to never run out of material for if I look at myself through the lens of humor, there are plenty of laughs ahead.

To live love, light, and laughter, I needed to pay attention. I cultivated objectivity through writing and I opened up to help, paying attention to what was happening so I could recognize it when it came. And I felt thankful, for all the help I got and continue to get.

Writing

"If a man is crossing the river and an empty boat collides with his skiff, even though he is a bad-tempered man he will not become very angry. But if he sees a man in the other boat he will scream and shout and curse at the man to steer clear. If you can empty your own boat crossing the river of the world, no one will oppose you, no one will seek to harm you. Thus is the perfect man: his boat is empty" (Chuang-Tzu).

Believe me, I am not the perfect man as described above, but I do strive to empty my boat. Writing allows me to do this, beginning with recognizing what is in the boat. It's usually not what I know that hurts me; it is what I don't know or the stories I tell myself about what's happening—stories with repetitive themes that I often confuse with the truth.

In order to write, like any practice it needs its designated place. There is a place in the front of my house, separated from the family room by a wooden pocket door, where I chronicled the inner journey that followed the outer journey in Scotland. At this time, I sit comfortably in my writing chair on a warm summer day with a gentle breeze blowing through the open window, leafing through my travel journal and writing on my computer.

My office is in order; I have a new desk. It is mission style with clean and simple lines, replacing the kidney-shaped Danish modern one that looked good but was impractical with its curved edges that pressed on my wrists while I typed. After writing long-hand in my chair, I go to my desk to transfer my handwritten script onto the computer. My cabinet is cleaned out and papers are organized in files or baskets, reducing clutter. There is a window by my desk, plants thriving in front of it, and beautiful artwork on the walls. I feel safely held, nurtured in this environment. This is the kind of order I am seeking in my soul—a tidiness that comes from reviewing what is there, letting go of what is no longer needed and filing what I want to keep so I can find it when I need it or better yet assimilate it into who I am, transforming the parts into the wholeness of wisdom.

When my experiences are word-ripe, I can move them from the hidden but powerful region of my unconscious mind and bring them into the light of consciousness. Then, instead of going through life blindly bumping into the unknown parts of myself, I can see what is there and work with it. I can digest my life, to assimilate what will nourish me and eliminate the rest. Undigested life material breeds cynicism and guilt. It reinforces a propensity to brace myself for life's hardships, projecting the past into the future.

That is how I lost my love, light, and laughter. I expected life's outcomes to be different; then I rallied and threw tantrums and tried to force them to be how I thought they should be. They did not change for me, so I blamed myself and others—but mainly myself, which dried up the wellspring of life. How unlike the more effective method of imagining the future, trusting the process, and doing footwork while remaining open in quiet anticipation. Yes, life is hard, humans suffer; so it makes sense to engage in practices that decrease the suffering (or at least don't increase it).

When I fell into a bitter battle with life, I lost, for life is bigger than me and will always win. It was at this time that my hormones were changing and I was meeting a new chapter of my destiny in which the intensive phase of mothering on a personal level was ending and it was time for mothering on a broader community level to begin. It was a crisis, a threshold. I needed to practice new skills and release regrets about my shortcomings in order to move forward unencumbered by them.

When love, light, and laughter started to flow again in my life, outer circumstances had less impact. Writing was a way to practice noticing and detaching—the first of the five steps to freedom (see appendix). Writing is also a form of step five in which I notice and practice gratitude. The more I paid attention to what was happening, the more grateful I felt. As I was faithful to my practice of the five steps to freedom, positivity grew. I became able to observe life's events in an objective way, achieving greater equanimity than I had ever known or thought possible.

Firstly, I started laughing—and not only with my women friends, where it came easily. I laughed a lot: with colleagues, while walking the dog, alone, while sleeping (out loud, and it woke me up—seriously!). Perhaps it was something funny in my dreams or just the habit of laughing bubbling up at night, much like worrying could awaken my thinking brain. Sometimes while grappling with a challenging situation, I would wake up laughing at the absurdity of it. I read funny books and practiced retelling every joke I heard, even the ones that weren't funny. I laughed at my own jokes and behaviors, especially the odd ones. I stopped taking myself and life so seriously, and at the same time began honoring it in a way that I could not before I saw the humor in it.

Secondly, I did my best to bring hurts, character defects, and residual shame into the light. In the light of consciousness, everything seemed to make sense. I deepened my practice of the Al-Anon program and my understanding of the philosophy of anthroposophy. This expanded my consciousness enough to embrace everything I had experienced, and motivated me to get up each morning and do my best, letting go of the rest. It provided a story that captured my imagination, so I could take responsibility for all aspects of my life and grow in community with others who are seeking the same things. I became a beginner, aware of what I did not know, open and committed to study and learn. The same thing happened with my yoga practice. I started all over again at a new yoga center, and in keeping with their protocol I worked my way through both physical and mental challenges on the mat, from level one to level three.

Finally, I gave up control and opened up to the flow of life, knowing that with love, light, and laughter, I could get through it all. Love, light, and laughter became the means and the goal, the medicine and the cure, the journey and the destination.

Life grew more interesting and full, fun and free—no matter what. Unconditionally, the fountain started flowing. It was not the promises, the allure of love, light, and laughter that got me going, though. It was the acute pain of life not working—of being so dried up and brittle that I was at risk of breaking. It was my parched soul that sent me looking for the fountain, and it was the fountain that allowed me to enter the flow again.

To mark my spiritual progress, I will shine the light of attention on my dog, my house, and my health, but believe me, the greatest impact was in my relationships with myself and those closest to me—thank God. Again, the story can be told using any part of the picture; every piece reflects the whole.

Training the Master

When Momma's not happy, nobody is happy. Mothers tend to set the emotional tone of the household—at least this held true in my family. How ironic that our dog was named Felice. My children were teenagers with a well-honed sense of irony at the time they named the dog. She was Miss Happy: full grown, one hundred and ten pounds of powerful, tail-wagging, I-want-to-make-you-really-happy energy. Energy that exaggerated my lack of dog-ease, frightened me, even paralyzed me sometimes. Energy it took me three years to learn how to manage. Or rather, it took me three years to realize I could not manage my dog, and one summer to learn to manage her by admitting that she was unmanageable, then asking for help, and then practicing what the trainer taught us.

When we hired the trainer she instantly fell in love with Felice, who responded to the trainer's unabashed, exuberant attention with her focused concentration. The trainer would walk with us up and down our street, coaching us in how to handle the dog and commenting on the beautiful houses and gardens. She made me aware of my alarmist reactions and gave me strategies, starting with ways to get Felice out of the door with me leading the way, setting off on the right foot. Everything started to click as soon as we started working the trainer's program. I've heard that before.

When we walked Felice, we led and she followed. She heeled. When we saw another dog, we kept her attention on us with verbal rewards and treats. She wouldn't lunge or bark if we managed her appropriately. We could restore our status in the neighborhood even when we walked by the houses where barking dogs lived. Those are the dogs that reminded us to keep Felice on leash. They bark fiercely every time we walk by. When we do, Felice looks at me and accepts a treat.

At this moment, Felice is sleeping in a ray of sunlight right by my desk. Her bark and her presence still scare people, and she may never be a dog that can sniff at another dog whether on or off leash. We accept that and love her anyway, poor social skills and all. When guests come over, she settles down quickly. (She still gets tail-wagging excited when our daughter visits, though. She rolls over, belly up, ready to be petted and scratched.) She is one big attention-seeker who pays attention to us most of the time now.

Anything we pay attention to expands in our lives. We learned to give attention to the behaviors that we wanted to reinforce in Felice, rather than inadvertently reinforcing the negative ones with our reactions. According to Goethe, "we are shaped and formed by what we love." Attention is a skill associated with love and so we are formed by what we pay attention to. We attend to what is before us, we tend to what needs to be done, and that is how we spread our love in the world. Love is more than feelings; it's a bundle of skills.

With Felice, it was very important that she pay attention to us. It is a two-way street. By attending to her behaviors and cues, we were able to garner her attention even when she was in the presence of a powerful distraction like another dog. One day, she may tune in to us enough that she can stay on leash and visit another dog without barking, lunging, or any other defensive posture. I'm going to hold that thought, and meanwhile accept what is and continue to master the dog-owner skills.

If Felice had not joined us, I doubt I would take as many long walks as I do. When I walk her, I see my neighbors out and about; I admire the houses and gardens along the way and sometimes the clouds, the sun, or the moon above. These walks connect me with nature and the community; they compel me to work with what is and accept what is not. Without attention, it's impossible to see what is there. This form of light radiates from our souls through our eyes with warm and objective interest.

I have learned to bring the light of attention to my relationship with Felice, to love her unconditionally (as she already loves us), and to address the behaviors I want to change—then laugh at her compulsions to sit on the couch or bark at dogs. Our relationship has evolved and will continue to grow; I am grateful for Felice and all that she has taught us.

Preparing for outings is a habit. Felice sits while I put the gentle lead over her snout. We pause before walking out the door. I lead the way with my best intentions and learned strategies. Felice follows. I praise her.

Building an Ark

My house and garden are a source of comfort, joy, and inspiration. The snapdragons and zinnias are blooming in the backyard alongside the herbs. Roses are up front. One bush is yellow and the other red. The rose of Sharon is full of pale pink blossoms in August, while the tiger lilies, hastas, and aromatic mint are everywhere and are past bloom. Sunflowers surround the maple tree with rocks defining the borders of their bed.

It has been both rainy and sunny almost every day this summer, which has kept the garden green and lush even when I neglected to water it. We have had to move outdoor parties onto the covered front porch, where there is a table, chairs, and lots of potted flowers. Summer showers breeze in and out again.

Inside the house, leaks kept coming for most of the summer. While we were away, the ceiling buckled near the edges and water flowed in and down onto the cookbooks, which then got moldy before we returned. We've had three roofers up there each doing a little more than the last. Finally, they tore off a huge section of the many layers of roofing, destroying two garden beds before replacing a large section of the roof. It took them a week to remove the old and put in a new roof. It was hot on the ground that week and even hotter on the roof, I can imagine. The roofers were loud, messy, and seemed to be everywhere. When they finished, I celebrated the quiet in my home and the chance to clean up my space both outside and inside.

When it rained, the roof did not leak. However, when my son took a shower that lasted long enough to test the plumbing and my patience, there was a puddle on the top shelf, which then dripped down onto lower shelves and then onto the floor. I put the cookbooks that survived the first flood in the pantry, positioned water pitchers to catch the leak, and called a plumber. We no longer had a roof problem, but we did have a plumbing problem so we started showering downstairs. The plumber found a hole in the hundred-year-old iron pipe. He knocked it loose and then replaced it with new piping so the corner where the laundry, shower, and toilet water flowed downstairs was repaired. Then my son took a shower. This time the ceiling in the hall closet caved in, drywall and water cascading down on the coats hanging there. Apparently when the plumber knocked one end of the pipe, the other end loosened—the one the shower water flowed into.

Ha! Floods everywhere: inside, outside, roof, pipes, closets. Clothes were soaked, and by the time they were moved to the pantry, the cookbooks were already ruined. There was no shortage of water around here and it was demanding our attention. Perhaps we needed to build the biblical ark which would hold us all and any animals we brought aboard. In a way, I think the practice of love, light, and laughter was my way of building an ark. That's what will carry us to higher ground and keep us safe from the deluge.

With the plumbing repaired, we were ready to repair the collateral damage to the kitchen ceiling and the closets in the back hall and upstairs next door to the bathroom where the problem started. We made it through the process and completed the work within the one-year commitment I made to love, light, and laughter. Yes: the plumbing and the people in the house are in better shape now than we have been in a long time. The kitchen shelves have a new coat of paint and I am grateful that my husband did the work involved in plugging the leaks.

I have to use humor in dealing with my old house. My garden is whimsical; the art that is hanging on our walls is largely local. We have a collection of primitive sculptures and I like to keep it fun. In the kitchen there is a painting by

Botero, the Colombian artist who paints people ever round and happy, even Mona Lisa. I find his work funny and up-lifting. I could not stop giggling when we visited the museum of his work in Bogota, Colombia. I want a happy house, one that people find lightness in. It is colorful and plant-filled; it is my canvas and there is always room to create in it.

Now when I walk into my house or any other house, I can appreciate it for what it is and refrain from making comparisons. It took me a long time to develop a healthy relationship with my house. There will always be more that I can do. I will attend to the emergency repairs as they come up and make cosmetic improvements as time and energy allow. I'll remember my objective is to make my house fun and comfortable and I will not worry about what it is not. I know what it is. I also know we can resolve any problems that arise and I know that they will. We love it and are committed to attending its messages and tending to our home, come what may.

Health and Balance

My naturopath diagnosed a yeast problem and suggested a special diet to avoid anything that feeds yeast, including all sugar products, alcohol, and even fruit for a while. I was finding all kinds of interesting things to eat. I tried making cookies with coconut oil one night, and the next night we went out to dinner. When we got home, I was still hungry, so I put some mochi (a fermented rice product that puffs up when baked) in the oven.

The kitchen filled with smoke. When I opened the oven door, there were flames inside. I considered not telling my husband since he would probably point out that I had not used the right baking sheet, which meant coconut oil had dripped onto the oven floor. I had made the same mistake the day before with the cookies.

"Honey, come see what is going on in the oven," I said while searching for the baking soda. That was not enough to arouse his attention, so then I said, "Help me put out the fire in the oven!" He came quickly and used a towel to swat the flames while I searched for the baking soda and then poured it into the oven. I heard about the baking sheets. Then I laughed about the whole business—the fire, the baking sheets, the way we have fallen into habits of communicating that have put our attention in the wrong place. Why did I make the same mistake? What was I paying attention to? Was I listening to the messages life was sending me? In order to learn, I needed to be patient, humble, and willing. Impatience and pride were obstacles to learning. A continual work in progress, I admit my defects; and when I do, I feel a sense of relief.

After four weeks on the sugar-free diet, I started eating

fruits and grains, and my symptoms returned. I went back on the diet for two more weeks and then slowly added in foods that I had been avoiding, paying attention to my body's reaction. Observing my emotional attachment to food helped me learn to detach, to pay attention without the emotion. My barometer was the rash on my hand, a biofeedback system. My skin was rash-free after my second try and it stayed clear even when I sampled wines on the west coast during our vacation. I exercise caution now, and I know how to read my body's signals most of the time.

I am aware of what I need to do to say healthy. It's bigger than what I eat and do but it includes that. I know I definitely need to laugh; by laughing I detach. When I celebrated a birthday with women friends, I was given a card with Gilda Radner on the front in the Rosanne Rosanna-danna character. When you open the card, there is a litany of complaints in the character's nasal monotone voice. All ten women at the table held the card and we laughed heartily as each one opened it and mouthed the words. I get it. Laugh at your pain—you will have a constant source of material. Don't take it all so seriously.

Everything that happens in my life is useful and if I cannot perceive its usefulness, I need to bring it into the light. By bringing life's circumstances into the light, I can live with them and I can work with them. I can transform my suffering into strength, and my fear into love.

That is the beginning and the ending. I have had to learn to love this life and the people and circumstances I encounter, and to give it my best. My best comes from my heart. It is my ability to love in spite of perceived mistakes and faults of my own and others. If I trust in life, I stay open to love and can then reap the benefits of peace and harmony that are promised by every wisdom path when we engage in the recommended practices.

There will be darkness in each day; my goal is not to rid my world of darkness. Instead, I practice finding the light, then my fear of the dark goes away and I am given the strength to meet whatever comes.

When I sit at the computer now, I have several other things calling for my attention, but if I take note of my physical body, my feelings, and my thoughts, I can fill the page before me and empty my head in order to make room for new thoughts.

Epilogue

Self must be Lord of self.
What other Lord should there be?

—*The Drammapada*

Acknowledging life and karma both as teacher and personalized curriculum points to the futility of comparing our circumstances with others. How could I have the same circumstances as another? I have different lessons presented through the curriculum of life's circumstances. Understanding this concept removes shame and embarrassment, impediments to learning. Once free of judgment about what I think should be happening, I can address what is.

Ultimately, I can benefit only from noting progress in my capacity to learn from life today compared with my capacity to learn from life yesterday. When I accept and work with karma's lessons, I am gifted with powers of lightness, peace and strength. These achievements are the true measures of success and the basis for all others. Without lightness in my thinking, peace in my heart, and strength in my will, outward achievement cannot create the happiness I seek. It's cultivating a healthy inner life that brings the most happiness and ability to serve my purpose in life.

Since I finished writing this work and have continued the practices described in it, I have found my next purpose in life. After parenting children in my home, I felt compelled to share what I had learned, to provide a place where children of working parents could be cared for. In the 1970s, my father would observe children being dropped off at child care while he was on his way to work. He was saddened by it. His children were home with their mother since it was not only possible for all of us to live on one income back then, but neighborhoods were set up in a way that supported families. A stay-at-home mom could find company in other stay-at-home moms and children could find friends to play with. We had siblings, neighbors, and accessible learning opportunities appropriate to an enriching early childhood experience.

Times have changed. There are more mothers working and no longer an established neighborhood network of support for families. LifeWays, the model for child care based on the work of Rudolf Steiner that I was trained in, is a form of new neighborhood. With knowledge of that model and the wishes of my father for home-like care for young children, I felt a strong sense of purpose. After emptying my own sack full of thoughts and feelings regarding my life so far, I was free and ready to take on something new, something big, something beyond what I have ever done before. With my experience, both personal and professional, and resources, as well as inspiration, I grew confident that I could open a LifeWays Center, a warm and nurturing environment where children could be cared for while their parents worked.

While this manuscript sat patiently on a shelf and I waited for the opportunity to revise it, I set to work founding a LifeWays Center. It developed into a successful being of its own, separate from me, and I am now free to pursue my writing again. The work fulfilled a deep purpose for me and brought me much joy, knowledge, and satisfaction. I am eternally grateful.

Do I wish that I had learned lessons earlier? This thought still shows up, but when it does, I recognize it. Telling myself that I should have learned something sooner than I did is a story, one that I can let go of.

I am still challenged regularly. There are more lessons to be learned. Overall, I am able to detach, be grateful for what is, and learn. What happened to my pet, my health, and my own home in the time I was creating the early childhood center, a home away from home for young children?

Felice got old and sick and developed trouble walking. Generally mellowed by age, she slept most of the day but still occasionally tugged on the leash when she saw another dog. Her body grew thin but her spirit stayed strong along with her desire to please us. On a warm summer day, when all she could do was sleep under the branches of the big fir tree, we had a veterinarian come to our house so we could say goodbye there. She let go peacefully, with dignity. In the end, after teaching me about leadership and love, she taught me to grieve, and I did.

My body has not blown up with yeast again but has brought other minor challenges that call for my attention. I realize that when I neglect to process my feelings consciously, my body often expresses them in one form or another. Today I have more energy and strength than I have ever had, while maintaining flexibility due to my yoga practice. My energy is like a battery that replenishes its power as long as I use it up during the day and restore it at night. Consistency in life habits and rhythms is fundamental. I forgive my body for illness, accidents, and scars; they brought moments of pause and useful lessons. I am grateful for the service my body has given me through the years.

When my mother passed away, her desk needed a new home and I welcomed it into mine. It is from the 1940s and is called a woman's desk. The dark wood is solid; it has eight drawers including one for files; it is streamlined and efficient, taking enough but not more space than is necessary. It supports me in creating flow and order in my work. There is a balance of feminine and masculine. I can honor the feminine, the inward or yin in my work while being contained by a masculine structure, by yang—solidity and form.

My house is overall orderly and comfortable with less urgent structural or cosmetic repairs calling for our attention. We are cleaning it out in preparation for selling it as soon as we have settled on a new home. We would like to live in a small, modern apartment without the burden of home maintenance, allowing for new decor and greater ease in house cleaning. Although I enjoy doing it, there are other things I enjoy more. The less I have, the less there is to maintain, to take my attention away from what I value, what matters most to me. It is time to celebrate life, to harvest the fruits of what we have sown lifelong.

I work from home full time, writing and mentoring, sorting through my experiences and my accumulated possessions, retaining only what is valuable to me now. It's time to set up life with my soul setting the tempo and tone, a life aligned with what I value.

I appreciate my husband's open spirit, excellent cooking skills, and expansive vision. He takes me to places I would never go on my own. Our adult daughter works in the early childhood center that I founded and will soon be a mother. Our son works in the family business. They both came to the work based on their personal process of choosing a life path. I accept them and love them wholeheartedly. I am proud of who they are and who they are becoming.

With them, I lead by example, for the years of teaching

them directly are over. They have their own karmic paths to follow and their own mission and purpose to fulfill. Do I wish at times that I had known what I know now so that I could have given them clear guidance when it was my job to do so? Yes I do, and when those feelings come up, I acknowledge them and then remember what I know about karma. The curriculum is a custom fit and I cannot alter it, only learn what comes when it comes. By detaching, I am able to practice self-forgiveness and trust karma, refraining from being an obstacle on anyone's karmic path—including my own. The more I accept my own karmic path and learning curve, the more acceptance and compassion I have for others.

When I claim a lesson learned, in order to keep it I must share it—which brings me full circle, turning a fragmented experience into a whole one.

As is often noted, challenging times can lead the way to our greatest successes. Karma presents lessons to learn what we need to know to achieve what we are meant to achieve. There are no mistakes—only gifts in the form of unlearned lessons. Why increase my own suffering by complaining, telling self-disparaging stories, or feeling guilty? If I make a mistake, I clean up it up and move on. Guilt lingers only if I don't clean up a mess I've made. Otherwise, mistakes serve as a reminder to act in keeping with my values and intentions, to do no harm. Once the message is heeded, the messenger is dismissed.

I am aware and accept that I learned codependent behaviors in childhood and did not unlearn and replace them until I had already passed the patterns on to my children. That is my primary regret. Given that set of circumstances, I am grateful that I chose to unpack the guilt of codependence and to repack my bags with honesty and confidence in my inner authority. With these tools I become the author of my own life, writing the story of a future that does not look like the past, finding freedom from what once defined and confined me.

While I wonder what will happen next, I trust life and that makes all the difference. Too late smart, I wonder? Or just the right time.

Appendix

Five Steps to Freedom

1. Pause. Notice your thoughts, feelings, and actions. Then create distance from them by removing yourself—physically, if possible. If not, remove yourself emotionally and mentally by detaching from feelings and thoughts, writing them down, and then allowing them to move through you. Notice the separation between yourself and your thoughts; they do not define you.

2. Place your hand on your heart. Ask yourself: Where is love missing here? You might be withholding love from yourself because you are having this uncomfortable experience. Consciously open up to the universal force of love and picture your heart glowing with it.

3. Place your hand on your forehead. Ask yourself: Where is the light of goodness in this situation? Then clear your mind and wait for the light to shine in, allowing fresh perceptions to appear while noticing any habitual limiting concepts. Know that good can be revealed in every situation.

4. Place your hand on your belly. Ask yourself: How can I see the humor in this situation? Whether you see the humor or not, start to laugh until your belly shakes, releasing stress from the physical body.

5. Notice your body, mind, and soul and the flow of energy you are experiencing. Give gratitude for all that is in your life. Remain open to signs of the impact of these steps in your relationships, especially the one with yourself. Whenever you notice something new and positive, give thanks for it. Stay conscious, awake.

Karma

"Zarathustra goes to the grave with the unfulfilled dreams of his youth. He speaks to them as if they were ghosts who have betrayed him bitterly. They struck up a dance and then spoiled the music. Did the past make his path so weighty? Did his unlived life impede him and consign him to a life that seems not to pass?"   —*Nietzche*

"Life is an echo. What you send out, comes back. What you sow, you reap. What you give, you get. What you see in others, exists in you."   —*Zig Ziglar*

"The law of karma is neither fatalistic nor punitive; nor is man a hapless, helpless victim in its bonds."

—*J.P. Vaswani*

"Karma is like the fruit of a mango tree. The mango will yield the tree and the tree will yield the mango and the cycle continues."   —*Niruben Amen*

"Between stimulus and response, there is a space. In that space is our power to choose our response. In our response lies our growth and our freedom."   —*Viktor E. Frankl*

"While we may judge things as good or bad, karma doesn't. It's a simple case of like gets like. The ultimate balancing act, nothing more, nothing less."   —*Alyson Noel*

"One can travel the world and see nothing. To achieve understanding, it is necessary not to see many things, but to look hard at what you do see."   —*Georgio Morandi*

"Karma is God's girlfriend."   —*Allan Williams*

"Develop a mind that functions freely, without depending on anything or any place."   —*Diamond Sutra*

"When you have the precious present, you will be perfectly content to be where you are."   —*Spencer Johnson, M.D.*

"There is a field beyond good and evil. I'll meet you there."
                                                        —*Rumi*

"Your proper concern is alone the 'action' of duty, not the 'fruits' of action. Cast then away all desire and fear for the fruits, and perform your duty."   —*Bhagavad Gita*

"Relax. Let go of urgency. Begin calmly now. Take one thing at a time."   —*The Language of Letting Go*

"If ever there is a tomorrow when we are not together, there is something you must always remember. You're braver than you believe, stronger than you seem, and smarter than you think. But the most important thing is, even if we're apart… I'll always be with you."   —*Winnie the Pooh*

"I would feel more optimistic about a bright future for mankind if he spent less time proving that he can outwit Nature and more time tasting her sweetness and respecting her Seniority."   —*E. B. White*

"The black moment is the moment when the real message of transformation is going to come. At the darkest moment comes the light."   —*Joseph Campbell*

"I would guess if you ordered the same food from two different restaurants, one chef with a negative attitude and one chef with a positive attitude, you could really taste the difference in attitudes."   —*Harry Palmer*

"Stay at the center and let all things take their course."

—*Lao Tzu*

"Karma is our teacher. It teaches us to refine our behavior—
hopefully sooner rather than later."

—*What is Hinduism?*

"Every time you are tempted to react in the same old way,
ask if you want to be a prisoner of the past or a pioneer of
the future." —*Deepak Chopra*

Made in the USA
San Bernardino, CA
10 December 2019

61218680R00068